CREATE -A- UTOPIA

WRITING AN IDEALISTIC STORY

Written by Eleanor W. Hoomes, Ph.D

Cover Design and Text Illustration by Tara Campbell

ACKNOWLEDGEMENTS

A group of students in the Heard Enrichment Program (HEP) in Heard County, Georgia, who have worked with me for the past seven years, have been of immeasurable help in preparing and polishing *Create-a-Utopia*. When they were in fifth and sixth grades, we did the Create-a-Town unit. When they were tenth- and eleventh-grade students, we did the Create-a-Utopia unit. They have been willing—or mostly willing—creators, writers, and critics as I have tried the various activities in this teaching unit with them. A special thank-you goes to David Adamson, Shane Barber, Keith Cornelius, David Crowe, Shawn Dougherty, Jimmy Free, Roger Harrod, Bonita Jackson, Lea Jones, Amy McLain, Freda Richardson, Greg Rogers, William Toney, and Mickey Workman.

ISBN 1-56644-014-9

Printed in the U.S.A.

EDUCATIONAL IMPRESSIONS, INC.
Hawthorne, New Jersey 07507

Contents

NOTE: A duplicate set of student worksheets is provided. These perforated pages, which appear at the back of the book, may be detached for photocopying for use by the buyer in the classroom. This allows the teacher to keep the set of Teacher Directions and Student Pages side by side in the book.

Introduction to the Teacher

Students like to create, write, and share stories; however, they can be baffled and become resentful when told to write a short story without being shown how to write one. Not knowing where nor how to begin, much less how to develop and end, they often write one skimpy paragraph and call it a short story. Conversely, when they are led through the structure of a story step by step, they often surprise themselves with the results.

Wise teachers capitalize on popular culture in the classroom. They begin with what is already familiar and interesting to students and use that knowledge and interest as springboards to introduce new knowledge. *Create-a-Utopia: Writing an Idealistic Story* builds on the existing knowledge of and interest in making our world a better place in which to live.

UTOPIA: An ideal fictional world where the inhabitants exist under perfect conditions. Impossible? In reality, maybe, but in fiction, no. Students as early as upper elementary school age are capable of visualizing a more perfect world than the one in which they live. With competent direction of a creative teacher who can channel their idealism and creativity and temper that idealism and creativity with just enough realism, students even at this early age are capable of constructing utopias. Older students will also need guidance in dealing with the complex issues raised by the utopian concept.

Included in *Create-a-Utopia* is a special introductory section, Create-a-Town, which works especially well with students in grades 4 to 9. It works in both social studies and language arts classes. Create-a-Town and Create-a-Utopia can be tied together in one unit, or they can be used as complete units individually.

The study of utopias makes an excellent springboard to the study of a variety of subjects—values, the nature of man, the future, sociology, history, the nature of reality, philosophy, and the nature of creative imagination; however, *Create-a-Utopia* uses the utopian ideals to encourage students to be creative, especially in writing.

Children can write—some better than others, of course, but they all have the raw materials needed for creative writing floating around in their lives. *Create-a-Utopia* is designed to bring order to those raw materials, help students sort and arrange that which is already familiar, and use the results to create stories. In the process of creating their stories, students will examine, discuss, and learn many new concepts. The by-products can be as rewarding as the finished stories. *Create-a-Utopia* may be used as a creative-writing unit, or it may be used in conjunction with a unit on utopian literature. With only a few modifications, it can be used with grades 4 through 12.

Create-a-Utopia will help develop students' abilities in observing, concluding, recalling, applying, analyzing, synthesizing, evaluating, divergent thinking, and convergent thinking. At the same time it will contribute to the development of their oral, written, and imaginative skills, with the additional advantage of being fun. Finally, it can give students a final product of which they can be proud!

The unit is designed to save thinking time and preparation time for teachers and to encourage planned creativity. Some teachers neither need nor want minute descriptions of teaching approaches and objectives while other teachers, because of time limitations, need more detailed instructions. All are capable of modifying an idea to suit their own purposes, and most prefer to innovate rather than copy; therefore, teachers may use *Create-a-Utopia* any way they wish, with only their imaginations limiting the various possibilities.

Behavioral objectives are not included because they are too precise and lengthy to include in a teaching unit of this type. Activities #9, #10, and #12 can be used as a bibliography.

I hope that this unit will be as educational and as much fun for other teachers and students as it has been for my students and me. Please contact me through Educational Impressions, Inc., Hawthorne, New Jersey, if you have any comments or questions about *Create-a-Utopia*. If you and your students enjoy using this book, you might also like to examine the other books in the Create-a-Story Series: *Create-a-Sleuth, Create-a-Monster, Create Heroes and Villains, Create-a-Future, Create-a-Comedy, Create-an-Autobiography* and *Create-a-Fantasy*.

Good luck!

Eleanor Wolfe Hoomes

NOTE: To increase the usefulness of this book, a duplicate set of student worksheet pages are provided. These perforated pages, which appear at the back of the book, may be detached for photocopying for use by the buyer in the classroom. This allows the teacher to keep the set of Teacher Directions and Student Work Sheets side by side in the book.

Create-a-Town

Create-a-Town

Activity No. 1, A–E   **Teacher Directions**

Objectives: To assist students in developing the component parts of a town

To help students to select a time and a place and to understand the limitations as well as the possibilities of those choices

To encourage students to work together

Thinking Skills: Observation

Recall

Application

Analysis

Divergent Thinking

Convergent Thinking

Synthesis

Evaluation

Directions: Activity No. 1, A-E, should be worked as a whole-group activity.

First discuss the characteristics of a town. Then tell students that they will create their own town, create characters for their town, and then write stories about their characters using their town as the setting. Next, work through the activities, one at a time. Because the questions are generally broad, you and your students might like to make them more specific or even to add more questions. If there is a disagreement, discuss the issues and then vote. Each student should keep notes.

A map will be a valuable tool—a large one that everyone can see or a small, easily-duplicated one. You might like to assign the best art students the task of mapmaking.

Setting

Activity No. 1, A   **Student Work Sheet**

The setting of a story includes both time and place. In Activity No. 1, A, of **Create-a-Town** you will determine when and where your story will take place. You have three choices in time—past, present, or future. If you choose the past, some research will probably be necessary. The world is the limit in choosing a place. If a "foreign" location is chosen, however, research will be necessary in order to "keep the facts straight."

Where is your town located? How large is it? Who are its neighbors? Why have you chosen this spot?

_____

_____

_____

_____

_____

_____

_____

When is the story happening? Are you using multiple times? For instance, are you setting your story in the present, but giving some history of the place? If so, explain.

_____

_____

_____

_____

_____

_____

_____

_____

_____

Government

You will deal mainly with local government in creating your town. Who are the elected officials? What are their jobs? Who are the appointed officials? How are they appointed? What types of local courts exist? How is revenue collected? What services, such as water, waste disposal, fire protection, etc., are provided by the government? How? Describe the law enforcement system.

_____

_____

_____

_____

_____

_____

_____

_____

_____

_____

_____

_____

_____

_____

_____

_____

_____

_____

_____

_____

_____

Industry and Business

Activity No. 1, C

Student Work Sheet

Industries and businesses not only provide goods and services to a community, but also provide jobs. What are the major industries and businesses in your town? How do they work together for the welfare of the community?

_____

_____

_____

_____

_____

_____

_____

_____

_____

_____

_____

_____

_____

_____

_____

_____

_____

_____

_____

_____

_____

Education and Recreation

Activity No. 1, D

Describe the educational system, starting with pre-school and going all the way to post-secondary (technical and vocational schools, colleges, and universities).

_____

_____

_____

_____

_____

_____

_____

_____

What kinds of recreational facilities (pools, lakes, tennis courts, gyms, baseball and softball diamonds, golf courses, camping facilities, parks, etc.) are available? How are they operated and maintained? Which are "free" to the public?

_____

_____

_____

_____

_____

_____

_____

_____

_____

_____

_____

Educational Impressions, Inc.

Transportation and Religion

Activity No. 1, E   **Student Work Sheet**

Describe the transportation network. What kinds of roads and streets are there? Who builds and maintains them? Is there a railroad? Airport? Is there a public transportation system? How is freight moved?

_____

_____

_____

_____

_____

_____

_____

_____

Describe the various religions which are practiced in your town. Where are the places of worship located? How are they built? Do the religions provide special programs? If so, what are they? What roles do the various religious organizations play in your town?

_____

_____

_____

_____

_____

_____

_____

_____

_____

Create-a-Town: Characters

Activity No. 2, A–E

Teacher Directions

Objectives: To guide students in determining the characteristics of their main characters and supporting characters

To encourage students to analyze the ramifications of assigning certain qualities to their characters

To provoke students to question initial reactions based on superficial qualities

Thinking Skills: Observation

Recall

Application

Analysis

Divergent Thinking

Convergent Thinking

Synthesis

Evaluation

Directions: Activity No. 2, A-E, should be worked individually.

Students will be creating main characters and supporting characters. Make sure that students understand the limitations and possibilities of assigning certain qualities to their characters. Also check to make sure students are not duplicating characters. For instance, there should be no more than one mayor, police chief, or fire chief; however, there could be as many barbers as the town could support.

Options: Stereotypes

Symbols

Decision-making

Educational Impressions, Inc.

Name, Physical Description, and Interests

Activity No. 2, A   **Student Work Sheet**

You are now going to create a main character and then supporting characters to inhabit the town you helped create in Activity No. 1.

The sex, age, race, dress, family, occupation, values, size, shape, personality, interests, and even name help determine not only how readers respond to a character but also how the character perceives himself/herself, how he/she behaves, and how other characters respond to him/her. Think through what you want your main character and supporting characters to be and do before you answer the questions in Activity No. 2, A–E.

What is the name of your character? _____

Age? _____ Sex? _____ Ethnic Background? _____

How long has the character lived in this town? _____

Where does the character live? Has the character always lived at this same address? _____

_____

What is the physical description of the main character? Include size, coloring, hair, eyes, and distinguishing marks and features. How does the main character dress? Draw and label your main character on another sheet of paper.

_____

_____

_____

_____

What are his/her hobbies and interests? _____

_____

Does he/she have any pets? If so, what are they and what are their names? How did he/she acquire the pets?

_____

_____

_____

Personality

Activity No. 2, B

What kind of personality does your main character have?

_____

_____

_____

What kind of speech does your main character use? Does he/she use slang? Proper English? Long words? Dialect? Clichés? Proverbs? Is the speech humorous and/or teasing, or is it serious?

_____

_____

_____

What special likes and dislikes does your main character have? How do his likes and dislikes affect his/her behavior?

_____

_____

_____

_____

What kinds of peculiar traits, habits, and/or gestures are common to your main character?

_____

_____

_____

_____

What phobias, if any, plague your main character? Why and how?

_____

_____

_____

_____

_____

Educational Impressions, Inc.

Occupations, Values, Strengths, & Weaknesses

Activity No. 2, C

Student Work Sheet

Many people derive their identity from their work. For instance, if you ask a person what he or she does for a living, the response will probably be, "I am a dentist (or a teacher, a carpenter, etc.)," rather than, "I do _____." Children, to some extent, are also identified by their parents' work—the minister's son or the principal's daughter. What is the occupation of your main character? Why do you choose this occupation for your main character?

_____

_____

_____

_____

What does your main character value? How will your main character's values affect his/her actions?

_____

_____

_____

_____

_____

What special strengths might your main character possess? How are they used? What are their limitations? How can these special abilities contribute to the successes of your main character?

_____

_____

_____

_____

What weaknesses might your main character possess? How might these weaknesses contribute to the problems faced by your main character?

_____

_____

_____

Motivation and Adventures

Activity No. 2, D   **Student Work Sheet**

What motivates your main character? How does your main character deal with his/her motivations?

_____

_____

_____

_____

_____

_____

_____

_____

What adventures might your main character have? What kinds of things might he/she do that would make a story interesting?

_____

_____

_____

_____

_____

_____

_____

_____

_____

_____

Family and Friends

Activity No. 2, E   **Student Work Sheet**

Who will be the supporting characters for your main character? Draw from his/her family and friends for additional characters. A phone directory is a big help in naming characters.

What kind of family does your main character have? How is family important to your main character? How might family members help or hinder your main character? List family members and explain their roles in your main character's life. Also give information about the home conditions of your main character.

_____

_____

_____

_____

_____

_____

_____

_____

_____

_____

What kinds of friends does your main character have? How are they important? List friends and explain their roles in your main character's life.

_____

_____

_____

_____

_____

_____

_____

_____

_____

_____

Create-a-Town

Activity No. 3

Teacher Directions

Objectives: To assist students in developing situations and plots for their stories

To encourage students to create detailed and believable situations and plots

To help students analyze the choices they make so that they understand the limitations and possibilities of each choice

Thinking Skills: Observation

Recall

Application

Analysis

Divergent Thinking

Convergent Thinking

Synthesis

Evaluation

Directions: Students should be paired for Activities 3 and 4. Groups of three or four could also be used. These two activities can be worked individually, but the results are usually not as rich.

In Activity No. 3 students will be developing situations and plots for their stories. Make sure that students thoroughly understand the give-and-take of working together. It might even be necessary to rearrange some non-working partnerships.

Options: Famous writing partnerships (For example, the old Dick Van Dyke Show shows three writers—Rob, Sally, and Buddy—collaborating.)

Situation and Plot

Activity No. 3   **Student Work Sheet**

Using your created main character and the main character created by a classmate (or class-mates), create a situation and a plot for a story, which you will write together in Activity No. 4. Work in the supporting characters as needed. How do your main characters meet? Do they already know each other? If so, how?

_____

_____

_____

_____

How do they cooperate and/or conflict? How do they feel about each other?

_____

_____

_____

_____

Plot is the sequence of events in a story. Plot is the action—what happens first, then next, then next, then next, until the end. In the space below plot your story with your partner(s), listing the major events as they occur.

_____

_____

_____

_____

_____

_____

_____

_____

_____

_____

_____

Create-a-Town: Writing a Story

Activity No. 4

Teacher Directions

Objectives: To assist students in analyzing the parts of a short story

To teach students the construction of a short story

To encourage students in writing a story

Thinking Skills: Application

Analysis

Divergent Thinking

Convergent Thinking

Synthesis

Evaluation

Directions: The same students who worked together in Activity No. 3 will work together in Activity No. 4 because it is an extension of Activity No. 3.

Discuss: Why must a story have a beginning, a middle, and an end? What kinds of conflicts might your main characters encounter? How will the conflicts be resolved? Why would a reader be more intrigued by the use of brains to solve a conflict as opposed to the use of brawn?

Instruct students to write their stories. Cover any writing mechanics which are necessary, such as the use of direct quotations, tense, and point of view. After corrections have been made, have students share their stories aloud.

Options: Good vs. evil as a literary theme

Tone

Theme

Educational Impressions, Inc.

Writing a Story

Activity No. 4

Student Work Sheet

You and your partner(s) are now ready to write a story. Base it upon all the information which you and your partner(s) have compiled on creating characters, setting, situations, and plots. Treat this story as the first installment in a series of exciting adventures if you wish. Remember to use direct conversation and to depict action as it occurs. A short story has three major parts.

1. The beginning where the characters, setting and background, and situation(s) are introduced,

2. The middle where complications and conflicts arise (a series of complications and conflicts may be encountered here), and

3. The ending where the conflicts and complications are resolved.

If you intend to use your characters again, you must leave them alive at the end, in situations which resolve the conflicts and uncomplicate the complications. Then they are capable of appearing in later stories. If possible, use brains instead of brawn to settle problems.

Instead of, or in addition to, the story you might like to try one of the following. See Activity No. 8 for more details.

1. A radio script

2. A play

3. A poem

4. A song

5. A comic strip

6. A filmstrip

7. A cartoon

8. A newspaper, radio, or TV news story

Introduction to Create-a-Utopia

I recently used the following Create-a-Utopia unit with a group of tenth- and eleventh-grade students in an American Government class. I used the Create-a-Town unit with the same students when they were in the fifth and sixth grades. During the course of the year, we studied local, state, and national government through active participation at all three levels. At the same time we read eight books: *Lord of the Flies, Animal Farm, Looking Backward, Connecticut Yankee in King Arthur's Court, 1984, Brave New World, Watership Down,* and *The Pushcart War.* When we finished the eight books, I divided the students into groups of three. Groups of two or four would work just as well, but I had fifteen students. Together they constructed utopias—all quite different. The results were fascinating. Three of the five utopias were regressive instead of progressive. Students who did not wish to confront the problem of technology simply set their utopias in an earlier, simpler time.

The unit works as well in English, humanities, and language arts classes as in social studies classes. It can be done without students actually reading utopian and/or dystopian literature; however, some knowledge of utopian literature and its history is necessary.

The minds of thinkers of every age have been fascinated by the concept of a better world for people. Religions promised paradise, heaven, and life after death, but some people wanted a better earthly life. From Plato to Skinner writers and philosophers have attempted to create ideal worlds. (See Activity No. 9 for a partial listing of utopian literature.) In 1516 Sir Thomas More published *Utopia.* "Utopia" is a word compounded by More from the Greek words meaning "not" or "no" and "place." Literally, it means "nowhere." Today the word "utopia" is used to define an ideal commonwealth, especially as to laws, government, and social conditions. Most utopias describe the ideal government, but at the same time, they usually criticize the social and economic conditions of the writer's time.

More's utopia is an island kingdom; it is crescent-shaped and approximately 500 miles in perimeter. Located somewhere in the ocean near the Western Hemisphere, the island is divided into fifty-four shires. The government is relatively simple, but it is mainly patriarchal. Each year every thirty households choose a magistrate. The 200 magistrates become the Senate. There are twenty officers, each in charge of ten magistrates and their households. The magistrates elect a president from a list of four previously nominated by the people. The president holds the office for life unless he is suspected of wishing to become a dictator.

There are few laws. The few that are needed are very clear; therefore, the need for lawyers has been eliminated.

There is complete religious tolerance. Wars are fought only to punish aggressors or in defense. Mercenaries are hired to fight them. Violence, bloodshed, and vice have virtually been eliminated. Those who do stray, however, are made into slaves, who do the "dirty" work.

People willingly work six-hour days, without money as payment. Each person spends two years working on a farm. All goods are community owned. Food is distributed from community dining halls and public markets. There is ample time for leisure and recreational pursuits.

Educational Impressions, Inc.

The communities are clean, buildings are beautiful, and the grounds are beautifully planted and well tended. There are good hospitals, humane prison systems, and planned parenthood.

Education is required for all, and everyone learns agriculture and one other craft. Parents give over the rearing of the children, after their early years, to public authorities. The unusually talented are selected for training in the Academy of Learning.

Later utopias deal more with equality than earlier ones did, especially of the sexes.

Some Major Concerns of Utopias

1. Abolition of war and lasting peace,

2. Elimination of poverty and disease,

3. Equality of sexes, races, and sometimes generations,

4. Family structure,

5. Education,

6. The good of the individual balanced with the good of the community,

7. Propaganda and censorship, and

8. Distribution of wealth.

Some Assumptions Commonly Made by Utopias

1. Mankind is basically good, intelligent (as well as rational), and altruistic.

2. Rulers are just and can be trusted.

3. People are self-motivated and do not become bored.

4. Total happiness can be achieved by all; there is no dichotomy between the needs of the individual and the needs of society because the utopia is not opposed to freedom.

5. People can sufficiently foresee the future and prepare for it.

6. People can be conditioned; most problems can be rectified by the proper education.

7. The sole purpose of a utopia is the earthly welfare of its inhabitants.

Some Recurring Elements in Utopias

1. Crime and disease are almost non-existent. Poverty has been abolished.

2. "Fashion" and style are unimportant. Uniformity and simplicity in dress, furnishings, and architecture are the norm. Form follows function.

3. Excesses are eliminated; therefore, order and cleanliness are easier to maintain. Private property is avoided.

4. Children are the concern of the whole community; communal nurseries for the younger children and dormitories for the older ones are provided.

5. Fit bodies and good characters are stressed.

6. Sexes are equal.

7. Education is necessary for the maintenance and continuation of the utopia.

8. The good of the individual and the state are the same.

9. Population growth is controlled. There are also eugenic controls.

10. Everyone works willingly.

11. There is ample leisure time, which is used constructively.

Educational Impressions, Inc.

Discussion Questions

The following questions can be used before, during, or after working through the Create-a-Utopia unit.

1. Can people ever agree on what constitutes the perfect world? Why or why not?

2. What is happiness?

3. In order to inhabit a "perfect" world, people must behave in "perfect" ways. Is this possible? Why or why not?

4. Can man control all the factors necessary to achieve a utopia?

5. What are the differences between utopian and dystopian literature?

6. Dystopian, or antiutopian, literature distorts the utopian concept. *Lord of the Flies, Animal Farm, Brave New World,* and *1984* show the darker side of human nature. Do we need both dystopian and utopian literature? Explain.

7. Will people control technology or will technology control people? Explain.

8. Would people be willing to submerge their individuality to the extent needed to create a "perfect" world? Explain.

9. Would living in a utopia become boring? Why or why not?

10. What are some problems in the world today which could be solved in a utopia? How could they be solved?

Create-a-Utopia: Background

Activity No. 5, A–G

Teacher Directions

Objectives: To assist students in developing backgrounds for their utopias

To encourage students to create detailed and believable backgrounds

The help students analyze the choices they make so that they understand the limitations and possibilities of each choice

Thinking Skills: Observation

Recall

Application

Analysis

Divergent Thinking

Convergent Thinking

Synthesis

Evaluation

Directions: In Activity No. 5, A–G, students will be developing backgrounds for their utopias. You may choose for students to do this individually, in small groups, or as a whole-class activity. If you have not done so already, this is a good time to introduce divergent and convergent thinking in the form of brainstorming and evaluation.

Options: Why is the utopian idea declining? What historical, political, and social factors have led to a more pessimistic view of life in the middle and later parts of the 20th century as opposed to a more optimistic view of life during the 18th and 19th centuries? How does this trend affect your view of the future of man? Of yourself?

Why do we need the utopian concept?

Educational Impressions, Inc.

Background: Setting

Activity No. 5, A   **Student Work Sheet**

A story which describes an ideal world where the inhabitants exist under perfect conditions is called a utopia. Utopias are usually set forward in time, backward in time, or they are in some way isolated from our world of reality.

The setting (time and place) and the background in utopian literature is of primary importance. Details must be well developed and believable within the framework of the story. The following questions will help you create a setting and a background for your own utopia. Add questions if necessary.

Where is the utopia set? Why? You might wish to draw a map on the back of this page.

_____

_____

_____

When is the story happening? Why did you choose this time?

_____

_____

_____

If you are creating a new world, what is the weather, topography, ecology, flora, fauna, etc., like? If you are using an existing world or part of an existing world, locate it and describe it.

_____

_____

_____

_____

_____

_____

_____

_____

Background: History

What is the history of your utopia?

How and why did the utopia begin?

_____

_____

_____

_____

_____

How long has your utopia existed?

_____

_____

How have the citizens in your utopia solved problems?

_____

_____

_____

_____

_____

Does the utopia have any problems now? If so, how are they being solved?

_____

_____

_____

_____

_____

_____

_____

Educational Impressions, Inc.

Background: Society and Family

Activity No. 5, C   **Student Work Sheet**

What is the structure of the society?

_____

_____

_____

What is the family structure? What are the responsibilities of various family members? Or has some other social structure replaced the biological family as we know it? If so, explain.

_____

_____

_____

How are children produced and reared?

_____

_____

Where and how do people live? How is the cooking, the cleaning, the laundry, general maintenance, etc., handled?

_____

_____

_____

What is the relationship between the races? The sexes? The generations?

_____

_____

_____

What do people do in their leisure time? What are their recreations?

_____

_____

_____

Background: Education, Religion and Government

Activity No. 5, D

Student Work Sheet

How are people educated? For how long? For what purposes?

_____

_____

_____

_____

_____

_____

What is the role of religion?

_____

_____

_____

_____

_____

How are people governed? Describe the government, starting with the smallest unit and progressing to the largest unit. Include courts, revenue collection, law enforcement, and other services which might be provided or regulated by a government.

_____

_____

_____

_____

_____

_____

Educational Impressions, Inc.

Background: Technology

How advanced is technology? Health care? Explain.

_____

_____

_____

_____

_____

_____

What energy sources are used?

_____

_____

_____

_____

_____

_____

_____

_____

What means of transportation are used? Explain the transportation network.

_____

_____

_____

_____

_____

_____

_____

Background: The Individual and the Distribution of Wealth

Activity No. 5, F

Student Work Sheet

What is the role of the individual in your utopia?

_____

_____

_____

_____

_____

_____

_____

How do people "earn a living"?

_____

_____

_____

_____

_____

_____

How are goods and services distributed? What is used for "money"? How do people own property: privately, collectively, or some other way? Explain.

_____

_____

_____

_____

_____

_____

_____

Educational Impressions, Inc.

Background: Peace, Press, and Propaganda

Activity No. 5, G

Has lasting peace been achieved? If so, how?

_____

_____

_____

_____

Have poverty and disease been eliminated? If so, how?

_____

_____

_____

Is propaganda used? If so, how?

_____

_____

_____

What is the role of the press?

_____

_____

_____

Will you need a special vocabulary in your utopia? Will you be using made-up words which need an explanation? If so, list and define them.

_____

_____

_____

_____

_____

Create-a-Utopia:
Creating Characters

Activity No. 6, A–C   **Teacher Directions**

Objectives: To guide students in determining the characteristics of their main characters and supporting characters

To encourage students to analyze the ramifications of assigning certain
qualities to their characters

Thinking Skills: Observation

Recall

Application

Analysis

Divergent Thinking

Convergent Thinking

Synthesis

Evaluation

Directions: In Activity No. 6, A–C, students will be creating main characters and
supporting characters for their utopias. Make sure that students understand the limitations and possibilities of assigning certain qualities to
their characters.

Characters in utopias need not be as well-rounded as characters in other
types of fiction because the utopia itself is the "main character."

Options: Stereotypes

One-dimensional characterization

Literature of ideas as opposed to literature of action

The New World as the Promised Land

Space (or the Mind) as the Last Frontier

Creating Characters

Activity No. 6, A

The sex, age, race, dress, origin, occupation, values, size and shape, personality, and name help determine not only how a reader responds but also how the character behaves and how other characters respond to him/her. Think through what you want your main character (also called hero or heroine or protagonist) and supporting characters to be or do before you answer the following questions about characters. You might like to use yourself or a friend as the main character.

What is the name of your main character? _____

What is the sex of your main character? _____

How old is your main character? _____

What is the physical description of the main character? Include size, coloring, hair, eyes, etc.

_____

_____

_____

_____

_____

What kind of personality does your main character have? Include likes and dislikes, speech patterns, habits, gestures, peculiarities, and phobias (if any).

_____

_____

_____

_____

_____

What is the occupation of your main character?

_____

_____

_____

_____

More about Your Main Character

Activity No. 6, B

Student Work Sheet

How and why is the main character living in a utopia?

_____

_____

Does your main character have any special interests and/or hobbies? If so, what?

_____

_____

_____

What motivates the character?

_____

_____

_____

_____

What does the character value? How do these values affect his/her actions?

_____

_____

_____

_____

What are the special strengths and weaknesses of the character? How do they affect his/her actions?

_____

_____

_____

_____

Creating Supporting Characters

Activity No. 6, C

Student Work Sheet

Who will be the supporting characters in your utopia? Use the questions in Activity No. 6, A and B, as a guide in creating at least three supporting characters. You may wish to draw from family and friends. You may also wish to create an older authoritarian figure (a mentor, such as Dr. Leete in *Looking Backward)* to help explain how the utopia operates. Very often the main character is not a native of the utopia, but somehow has found his/her way into the utopia. Usually there is a person (with secondary help, of course) who shows him/her around and answers questions.

What kind of family does your main character have? List family members and explain their roles in his/her life.

_____

_____

_____

_____

_____

_____

_____

_____

List friends and/or mentors and explain their roles in your main character's life.

_____

_____

_____

_____

_____

_____

_____

_____

Create-a-Utopia: Plot and Story

Activity No. 7

Teacher Directions

Objectives: To guide students in plotting a story in sequence

To help students construct a story from the material they have compiled in Activities 5 and 6.

Thinking Skills: Observation

Recall

Application

Analysis

Divergent Thinking

Convergent Thinking

Synthesis

Evaluation

Directions: Help students in sequencing their stories. Refer to Teacher Directions for Activity No. 4 for additional suggestions.

Options: Outline the plot of a utopian, or another, book with which the students are already familiar. See Activity No. 9 for a partial listing of utopian literature.

Students might like to present their utopias to another class in choral reading or in a reader's theater.

Students might like to make copies of their utopias and bind them into a magazine.

Students might like to present their utopias to a parents group or to other adult groups in the community.

Discuss: Who are some utopian thinkers of today?

Educational Impressions, Inc.

Plot and Story

Activity No. 7

Student Work Sheet

Something must happen in a story. Plot is the sequence of happenings in a story. Plot is the action—what happens first, then next, then next, until the end. Plot in a utopia is generally secondary; the society and how it works is primary. Plot the sequence of events for the utopia you are creating.

_____

_____

_____

_____

_____

_____

_____

_____

_____

_____

_____

_____

_____

_____

_____

_____

_____

_____

_____

You are now ready to write your utopian story. Base it upon all the information which you have compiled in the previous activities. Do not present all of the details you have worked out in Activities 5 through 7 in the first part of the story. Work the information into the story as it progresses through dialogue, thoughts of the main character, and action.

Determine the point of view and the tense you will use in telling your story. Now, start writing. Remember, a good story is worth revising and rewriting!

Create-a-Utopia:
Alternatives to Writing a Short Story

Activities 8–12

Objectives: To provide alternatives to the writing of a short story

To provide opportunities for those students who wish to explore the utopian and dystopian concept in literature in more depth

To provide a list of utopian experiments so students can do historical research on selected communities

Thinking Skills: Observation

Recall

Application

Analysis

Divergent Thinking

Convergent Thinking

Synthesis

Evaluation

Other Ways to Use Utopias

Activity No. 8

Student Work Sheet

In addition to writing a short story, you may wish to try some of the following suggestions:

Write a radio script. With appropriate sound effects, the script may be produced for an audience by simply using a screen to conceal the participants from their audience. The script could also be recorded on a tape recorder and then played for the audience. Do not overlook the use of music to achieve dramatic effects.

Write a play. A play is not complete unless it is staged. Producing a play involves more work than producing a radio show because the audience sees the actors. Lines and actions must be learned; whereas, in a radio show the lines can be read. If you have access to a video camera, filming the play could be an interesting experience.

Draw a comic strip. Study comic books so you are thoroughly familiar with all the conventions of comic-book writing.

Write a narrative poem. Treat your material in either a serious or a humorous manner.

Write a song. Set it to music and record it on a tape recorder.

Draw a filmstrip of the story you wrote in Activity No. 9 or write a new story. Record the story on a tape recorder and synchronize the two to show to an audience.

Draw cartoons of your main character. Show him/her in situations which reveal characteristics of your utopia.

Write a newspaper article about the utopia. Use an eye-catching headline. Remember to answer the following questions: Who? What? Where? Why? When? How?

Turn your newspaper account into a TV news bulletin, a TV feature story, or an interview.

Utopian Literature

The following is a partial list of utopian literature:

Plato. *The Republic* (375? B.C.)

More, Thomas. *Utopia* (1516)

Bacon, Francis. *New Atlantis* (1627)

Campanella, Thomas. *City of the Sun* (1637)

Harrington, James. *Oceana* (1656)

Lytton, Bulwer. *The Coming Race* (1871)

Buttler, Samuel. *Erewhon, or Over the Range* (1872)

Bellamy, Edward. *Looking Backward* (1887)

              Equality (1897)

Morris, William. *News from Nowhere* (1892)

Wells, H.G. *Anticipations* (1901)

        A Modern Utopia (1905)

        New World for Old (1908)

Hilton, James. *Lost Horizon* (1933)

Hesse, Herman. *Magister Ludi* (1943)

         The Glass Head Game (1945)

Reynolds, Mack. *Looking Backward from the Year 2000* (1977)

         Equality in the Year 2000 (1977)

Nelson, Ray. *Then Beggars Could Ride* (1976)

Dystopian Literature

The following is a partial list of dystopian literature:

Asimov, Isaac. *Nine Tomorrows: Tales of the Near Future*

Boulle, Pierre. *Planet of the Apes*

Bradbury, Ray. *Fahrenheit 451*

Clarke, Arthur. *Childhood's End*

Graves, Robert. *Watch the Northwind Rise*

Hudson, W.H. *A Crystal Age*

Huxley, Aldous. *Brave New World*

                Ape and Essence

                Island

Karp, David. *One*

Levin, Ira. *This Perfect Day*

Lowry, Lois. *The Giver*

Miller, Walter M. *Canticle for Leibowitz*

Orwell, George. *Animal Farm*

                1984

Rand, Ann. *Anthem*

            Atlas Shrugged

Swift, Jonathan. *Gulliver's Travels*

Vidal, Gore. *Messiah*

Vonnegut, Kurt, Jr. *Player Piano*

Waugh, Evelyn. *Love Among the Ruins*

Wolfe, Bernard. *Limbo*

Utopian Communities

Activity No. 11

Student Work Sheet

The utopian idea moved to the United States during the last part of the 18th century and the first half of the 19th century. Many experimental communities were begun, but few were very long lasting. Below is an abbreviated list of a few of the communities which were started in America. Choose one of these (or add one of your own) and learn what you can about the community.

Ephrata (1732–1905)

Rappite Settlements (1803–1905)

   Community of Equality

   Harmony

   Economy

Amana Society (1843–1900s)

   Ebenezer and seven other communities

Shakers (1787–1900s)

   New Lebanon and seventeen other settlements in eight states

Oneida Community (1841–1879)

   New Harmony (1825–1827)

Fruitlands (19th century)

Brook Farm (19th century)

Morningstar (20th century)

Communes (mid-20th century)

Other ideas worth research are monasteries and convents, the Israeli kibbutzim and shitufim, and farm or other collectives.

Educational Impressions, Inc.

Dystopian Literature

Activity No. 10

Student Work Sheet

The following is a partial list of dystopian literature:

Asimov, Isaac. *Nine Tomorrows: Tales of the Near Future*

Boulle, Pierre. *Planet of the Apes*

Bradbury, Ray. *Fahrenheit 451*

Clarke, Arthur. *Childhood's End*

Graves, Robert. *Watch the Northwind Rise*

Hudson, W.H. *A Crystal Age*

Huxley, Aldous. *Brave New World*
> *Ape and Essence*
> *Island*

Karp, David. *One*

Levin, Ira. *This Perfect Day*

Lowry, Lois. *The Giver*

Miller, Walter M. *Canticle for Leibowitz*

Orwell, George. *Animal Farm*
> *1984*

Rand, Ann. *Anthem*
> *Atlas Shrugged*

Swift, Jonathan. *Gulliver's Travels*

Vidal, Gore. *Messiah*

Vonnegut, Kurt, Jr. *Player Piano*

Waugh, Evelyn. *Love Among the Ruins*

Wolfe, Bernard. *Limbo*

Utopian Communities

Activity No. 11   **Student Work Sheet**

The utopian idea moved to the United States during the last part of the 18th century and the first half of the 19th century. Many experimental communities were begun, but few were very long lasting. Below is an abbreviated list of a few of the communities which were started in America. Choose one of these (or add one of your own) and learn what you can about the community.

Ephrata (1732–1905)

Rappite Settlements (1803–1905)

   Community of Equality

   Harmony

   Economy

Amana Society (1843–1900s)

   Ebenezer and seven other communities

Shakers (1787–1900s)

   New Lebanon and seventeen other settlements in eight states

Oneida Community (1841–1879)

   New Harmony (1825–1827)

Fruitlands (19th century)

Brook Farm (19th century)

Morningstar (20th century)

Communes (mid-20th century)

Other ideas worth research are monasteries and convents, the Israeli kibbutzim and shitufim, and farm or other collectives.

Secondary Sources

Activity No. 12   **Student Work Sheet**

Amis, Kingsley. *New Maps of Hell*

Armytage, W.H.G. *Yesterday's Tomorrows*

Bailey, J.O. *Pilgrim's Through Time and Space: Patterns in Scientific and Utopian Fiction*

Berneri, Marie Louise. *Journey Through Utopia*

Erasmus, Charles J. *In Search of the Common Good: Utopian Experiments Past and Future*

Eurich, Neal. *Science in Utopia: A Mighty Design*

Gerber, Richard. *Utopian Fantasy*

Gray, Donald J. and Allan Orrick. *Designs of Famous Utopias: Materials for Research
     Papers*

Hertzler, Joyce O. *The History of Utopian Thought*

Manuel, Frank E. *Utopias and Utopian Thought*

Meyer, Karl E. *The New America: Politics and Society in the Age of the Smooth Deal*

Moos, Rudolph and Robert Brownstein. *Environment and Utopia: A Synthesis*

Mumford, Lewis. *The Story of Utopias*

Negley, Gleen and J. Max Patrick. *The Quest for Utopia: An Anthology of Imaginary
     Societies*

North, Robert C. *The World That Could Be*

Richter, Peyton E. *Utopias: Social Ideals and Communal Experiments*

Russel, Frances Theresa. *Touring America*

Walsh, Chad. *From Utopia to Nightmare*

Weisbrod, Carol. *The Boundaries of Utopias*

Tear-Out
Reproducible
Student
Work Sheets

Setting

Activity No. 1, A

Student Work Sheet

The setting of a story includes both time and place. In Activity No. 1, A, of **Create-a-Town** you will determine when and where your story will take place. You have three choices in time—past, present, or future. If you choose the past, some research will probably be necessary. The world is the limit in choosing a place. If a "foreign" location is chosen, however, research will be necessary in order to "keep the facts straight."

Where is your town located? How large is it? Who are its neighbors? Why have you chosen this spot?

_____

_____

_____

_____

_____

_____

_____

When is the story happening? Are you using multiple times? For instance, are you setting your story in the present, but giving some history of the place? If so, explain.

_____

_____

_____

_____

_____

_____

_____

_____

_____

_____

Government

Activity No. 1, B

Student Work Sheet

You will deal mainly with local government in creating your town. Who are the elected officials? What are their jobs? Who are the appointed officials? How are they appointed? What types of local courts exist? How is revenue collected? What services, such as water, waste disposal, fire protection, etc., are provided by the government? How? Describe the law enforcement system.

_____

_____

_____

_____

_____

_____

_____

_____

_____

_____

_____

_____

_____

_____

_____

_____

_____

_____

_____

Educational Impressions, Inc.

Industry and Business

Activity No. 1, C

Student Work Sheet

Industries and businesses not only provide goods and services to a community, but also provide jobs. What are the major industries and businesses in your town? How do they work together for the welfare of the community?

_____

_____

_____

_____

_____

_____

_____

_____

_____

_____

_____

_____

_____

_____

_____

_____

_____

_____

_____

_____

_____

_____

_____

_____

Education and Recreation

Activity No. 1, D

Student Work Sheet

Describe the educational system, starting with pre-school and going all the way to post-secondary (technical and vocational schools, colleges, and universities).

_____

_____

_____

_____

_____

_____

_____

_____

_____

What kinds of recreational facilities (pools, lakes, tennis courts, gyms, baseball and softball diamonds, golf courses, camping facilities, parks, etc.) are available? How are they operated and maintained? Which are "free" to the public?

_____

_____

_____

_____

_____

_____

_____

_____

_____

_____

Transportation and Religion

Describe the transportation network. What kinds of roads and streets are there? Who builds and maintains them? Is there a railroad? Airport? Is there a public transportation system? How is freight moved?

_____

_____

_____

_____

_____

_____

_____

_____

Describe the various religions which are practiced in your town. Where are the places of worship located? How are they built? Do the religions provide special programs? If so, what are they? What roles do the various religious organizations play in your town?

_____

_____

_____

_____

_____

_____

_____

_____

Name, Physical Description, and Interests

Activity No. 2, A

You are now going to create a main character and then supporting characters to inhabit the town you helped create in Activity No. 1.

The sex, age, race, dress, family, occupation, values, size, shape, personality, interests, and even name help determine not only how readers respond to a character but also how the character perceives himself/herself, how he/she behaves, and how other characters respond to him/her. Think through what you want your main character and supporting characters to be and do before you answer the questions in Activity No. 2, A–E.

What is the name of your character? _____

Age? _____ Sex? _____ Ethnic Background? _____

How long has the character lived in this town? _____

Where does the character live? Has the character always lived at this same address? _____

_____

What is the physical description of the main character? Include size, coloring, hair, eyes, and distinguishing marks and features. How does the main character dress? Draw and label your main character on another sheet of paper.

_____

_____

_____

_____

What are his/her hobbies and interests? _____

_____

Does he/she have any pets? If so, what are they and what are their names? How did he/she acquire the pets?

_____

_____

_____

Educational Impressions, Inc.

Personality

Activity No. 2, B

What kind of personality does your main character have?

_____

_____

_____

What kind of speech does your main character use? Does he/she use slang? Proper English? Long words? Dialect? Clichés? Proverbs? Is the speech humorous and/or teasing, or is it serious?

_____

_____

_____

What special likes and dislikes does your main character have? How do his likes and dislikes affect his/her behavior?

_____

_____

_____

_____

What kinds of peculiar traits, habits, and/or gestures are common to your main character?

_____

_____

_____

_____

What phobias, if any, plague your main character? Why and how?

_____

_____

_____

_____

Occupations, Values, Strengths, & Weaknesses

Activity No. 2, C

Many people derive their identity from their work. For instance, if you ask a person what he or she does for a living, the response will probably be, "I am a dentist (or a teacher, a carpenter, etc.)," rather than, "I do _____." Children, to some extent, are also identified by their parents' work—the minister's son or the principal's daughter. What is the occupation of your main character? Why do you choose this occupation for your main character?

_____

_____

_____

_____

What does your main character value? How will your main character's values affect his/her actions?

_____

_____

_____

_____

_____

What special strengths might your main character possess? How are they used? What are their limitations? How can these special abilities contribute to the successes of your main character?

_____

_____

_____

_____

What weaknesses might your main character possess? How might these weaknesses contribute to the problems faced by your main character?

_____

_____

_____

Educational Impressions, Inc.

Motivation and Adventures

Activity No. 2, D

Student Work Sheet

What motivates your main character? How does your main character deal with his/her motivations?

_____

_____

_____

_____

_____

_____

_____

_____

What adventures might your main character have? What kinds of things might he/she do that would make a story interesting?

_____

_____

_____

_____

_____

_____

_____

_____

_____

Family and Friends

Activity No. 2, E

Student Work Sheet

Who will be the supporting characters for your main character? Draw from his/her family and friends for additional characters. A phone directory is a big help in naming characters.

What kind of family does your main character have? How is family important to your main character? How might family members help or hinder your main character? List family members and explain their roles in your main character's life. Also give information about the home conditions of your main character.

_____

_____

_____

_____

_____

_____

_____

_____

_____

What kinds of friends does your main character have? How are they important? List friends and explain their roles in your main character's life.

_____

_____

_____

_____

_____

_____

_____

_____

_____

Educational Impressions, Inc.

Situation and Plot

Activity No. 3

Student Work Sheet

Using your created main character and the main character created by a classmate (or class-mates), create a situation and a plot for a story, which you will write together in Activity No. 4. Work in the supporting characters as needed. How do your main characters meet? Do they already know each other? If so, how?

_____

_____

_____

_____

How do they cooperate and/or conflict? How do they feel about each other?

_____

_____

_____

_____

Plot is the sequence of events in a story. Plot is the action—what happens first, then next, then next, then next, until the end. In the space below plot your story with your partner(s), listing the major events as they occur.

_____

_____

_____

_____

_____

_____

_____

_____

_____

Writing a Story

Activity No. 4

Student Work Sheet

You and your partner(s) are now ready to write a story. Base it upon all the information which you and your partner(s) have compiled on creating characters, setting, situations, and plots. Treat this story as the first installment in a series of exciting adventures if you wish. Remember to use direct conversation and to depict action as it occurs. A short story has three major parts.

1. The beginning where the characters, setting and background, and situation(s) are introduced,

2. The middle where complications and conflicts arise (a series of complications and conflicts may be encountered here), and

3. The ending where the conflicts and complications are resolved.

If you intend to use your characters again, you must leave them alive at the end, in situations which resolve the conflicts and uncomplicate the complications. Then they are capable of appearing in later stories. If possible, use brains instead of brawn to settle problems.

Instead of, or in addition to, the story you might like to try one of the following. See Activity No. 8 for more details.

1. A radio script

2. A play

3. A poem

4. A song

5. A comic strip

6. A filmstrip

7. A cartoon

8. A newspaper, radio, or TV news story

Educational Impressions, Inc.

Background: Setting

Activity No. 5, A   **Student Work Sheet**

A story which describes an ideal world where the inhabitants exist under perfect conditions is called a utopia. Utopias are usually set forward in time, backward in time, or they are in some way isolated from our world of reality.

The setting (time and place) and the background in utopian literature is of primary importance. Details must be well developed and believable within the framework of the story. The following questions will help you create a setting and a background for your own utopia. Add questions if necessary.

Where is the utopia set? Why? You might wish to draw a map on the back of this page.

_____

_____

_____

When is the story happening? Why did you choose this time?

_____

_____

_____

_____

If you are creating a new world, what is the weather, topography, ecology, flora, fauna, etc., like? If you are using an existing world or part of an existing world, locate it and describe it.

_____

_____

_____

_____

_____

_____

_____

_____

Background: History

Activity No. 5, B

Student Work Sheet

What is the history of your utopia?

How and why did the utopia begin?

_____

_____

_____

_____

_____

How long has your utopia existed?

_____

_____

How have the citizens in your utopia solved problems?

_____

_____

_____

_____

Does the utopia have any problems now? If so, how are they being solved?

_____

_____

_____

_____

_____

Educational Impressions, Inc.

Background: Society and Family

Activity No. 5, C

Student Work Sheet

What is the structure of the society?

_____

_____

_____

What is the family structure? What are the responsibilities of various family members? Or has some other social structure replaced the biological family as we know it? If so, explain.

_____

_____

_____

How are children produced and reared?

_____

_____

_____

Where and how do people live? How is the cooking, the cleaning, the laundry, general maintenance, etc., handled?

_____

_____

_____

What is the relationship between the races? The sexes? The generations?

_____

_____

_____

What do people do in their leisure time? What are their recreations?

_____

_____

_____

Background: Education, Religion and Government

Activity No. 5, D

Student Work Sheet

How are people educated? For how long? For what purposes?

_____

_____

_____

_____

_____

_____

What is the role of religion?

_____

_____

_____

_____

_____

How are people governed? Describe the government, starting with the smallest unit and progressing to the largest unit. Include courts, revenue collection, law enforcement, and other services which might be provided or regulated by a government.

_____

_____

_____

_____

_____

_____

Educational Impressions, Inc.

Background: Technology

Activity No. 5, E

Student Work Sheet

How advanced is technology? Health care? Explain.

_____

_____

_____

_____

_____

What energy sources are used?

_____

_____

_____

_____

_____

_____

_____

What means of transportation are used? Explain the transportation network.

_____

_____

_____

_____

_____

_____

Background: The Individual and the Distribution of Wealth

Activity No. 5, F

What is the role of the individual in your utopia?

_____

_____

_____

_____

_____

_____

How do people "earn a living"?

_____

_____

_____

_____

_____

_____

How are goods and services distributed? What is used for "money"? How do people own property: privately, collectively, or some other way? Explain.

_____

_____

_____

_____

_____

_____

_____

Educational Impressions, Inc.

Background: Peace, Press, and Propaganda

Activity No. 5, G   **Student Work Sheet**

Has lasting peace been achieved? If so, how?

_____

_____

_____

Have poverty and disease been eliminated? If so, how?

_____

_____

_____

Is propaganda used? If so, how?

_____

_____

_____

What is the role of the press?

_____

_____

_____

Will you need a special vocabulary in your utopia? Will you be using made-up words which need an explanation? If so, list and define them.

_____

_____

_____

_____

_____

Creating Characters

The sex, age, race, dress, origin, occupation, values, size and shape, personality, and name help determine how a character behaves, how other characters respond to him/her, as well as how a reader responds. Think through what you want your main character (also called hero or hero-ine or protagonist) and supporting characters to be or do before you answer the following questions about characters. You might like to use yourself or a friend as the main character.

What is the name of your main character? _____

What is the sex of your main character? _____

How old is your main character? _____

What is the physical description of the main character? Include size, coloring, hair, eyes, etc. How does he/she dress?

_____

_____

_____

_____

_____

_____

What kind of personality does your main character have? Include likes and dislikes, speech patterns, habits, gestures, peculiarities, and phobias (if any).

_____

_____

_____

_____

_____

What is the occupation of your main character?

_____

_____

_____

_____

Educational Impressions, Inc.

More about Your
Main Character

Activity No. 6, B

Student Work Sheet

How and why is the main character living in a utopia?

_____

_____

Does he/she have any special interests and/or hobbies? If so, what?

_____

_____

_____

What motivates the character?

_____

_____

_____

_____

What does the character value? How do these values affect his/her actions?

_____

_____

_____

_____

What are the special strengths and weaknesses of the character? How do they affect his/her actions?

_____

_____

_____

_____

Creating Supporting Characters

Activity No. 6, C

Student Work Sheet

Who will be the supporting characters in your utopia? Use the questions in Activity No. 6, A and B, as a guide in creating at least three supporting characters. You may wish to draw from family and friends. You may also wish to create an older, authoritarian figure, (a mentor, such as Dr. Leete in *Looking Backward)* to help explain how the utopia operates. Very often the main character is not a native of the utopia, but somehow has found his/her way into the utopia. Usually there is a person (with secondary help, of course) who shows him/her around and answers questions.

What kind of family does your main character have? List family members and explain their roles in his/her life.

_____

_____

_____

_____

_____

_____

_____

_____

_____

List friends and/or mentors and explain their roles in your main character's life.

_____

_____

_____

_____

_____

_____

_____

_____

_____

Educational Impressions, Inc.

Plot and Story

Something must happen in a story. Plot is the sequence of happenings in a story. Plot is the action—what happens first, then next, then next, until the end. Plot in a utopia is generally secondary; the society and how it works is primary. Plot the sequence of events for the utopia you are creating.

_____

_____

_____

_____

_____

_____

_____

_____

_____

_____

_____

_____

_____

_____

_____

_____

_____

You are now ready to write your utopian story. Base it upon all the information which you have compiled in the previous activities. Do not present all of the details you have worked out in Activities 5 through 7 in the first part of the story. Work the information into the story as it progresses through dialogue, thoughts of the main character, and action.

Determine the point of view and the tense you will use in telling your story. Now, start writing. Remember a good story is worth revising and rewriting!

Other Ways to Use Utopias

In addition to writing a short story, you may wish to try some of the following suggestions:

Write a radio script. With appropriate sound effects, the script may be produced for an audience by simply using a screen to conceal the participants from their audience. The script could also be recorded on a tape recorder and then played for the audience. Do not overlook the use of music to achieve dramatic effects.

Write a play. A play is not complete unless it is staged. Producing a play involves more work than producing a radio show because the audience sees the actors. Lines and actions must be learned; whereas, in a radio show the lines can be read. If you have access to a video camera, filming the play could be an interesting experience.

Draw a comic strip. Study comic books so you are thoroughly familiar with all the conventions of comic-book writing.

Write a narrative poem. Treat your material in either a serious or a humorous manner.

Write a song. Set it to music and record it on a tape recorder.

Draw a filmstrip of the story you wrote in Activity No. 9 or write a new story. Record the story on a tape recorder and synchronize the two to show to an audience.

Draw cartoons of your main character. Show him/her in situations which reveal characteristics of your utopia.

Write a newspaper article about the utopia. Use an eye-catching headline. Remember to answer the following questions: Who? What? Where? Why? When? How?

Turn your newspaper account into a TV news bulletin, a TV feature story, or an interview.

Utopian Literature

Activity No. 9

The following is a partial list of utopian literature:

Plato. *The Republic* (375? B.C.)

More, Thomas. *Utopia* (1516)

Bacon, Francis. *New Atlantis* (1627)

Campanella, Thomas. *City of the Sun* (1637)

Harrington, James. *Oceana* (1656)

Lytton, Bulwer. *The Coming Race* (1871)

Buttler, Samuel. *Erewhon, or Over the Range* (1872)

Bellamy, Edward. *Looking Backward* (1887)

                       Equality (1897)

Morris, William. *News from Nowhere* (1892)

Wells, H.G. *Anticipations* (1901)

                A Modern Utopia (1905)

                New World for Old (1908)

Hilton, James. *Lost Horizon* (1933)

Hesse, Herman. *Magister Ludi* (1943)

                The Glass Head Game (1945)

Reynolds, Mack. *Looking Backward from the Year 2000* (1977)

                Equality in the Year 2000 (1977)

Nelson, Ray. *Then Beggars Could Ride* (1976)

Dystopian Literature

Activity No. 10

Student Work Sheet

The following is a partial list of dystopian literature:

Asimov, Isaac. *Nine Tomorrows: Tales of the Near Future*

Boulle, Pierre. *Planet of the Apes*

Bradbury, Ray. *Fahrenheit 451*

Clarke, Arthur. *Childhood's End*

Graves, Robert. *Watch the Northwind Rise*

Hudson, W.H. *A Crystal Age*

Huxley, Aldous. *Brave New World*

              Ape and Essence

              Island

Karp, David. *One*

Levin, Ira. *This Perfect Day*

Lowry, Lois. *The Giver*

Miller, Walter M. *Canticle for Leibowitz*

Orwell, George. *Animal Farm*

              1984

Rand, Ann. *Anthem*

          Atlas Shrugged

Swift, Jonathan. *Gulliver's Travels*

Vidal, Gore. *Messiah*

Vonnegut, Kurt, Jr. *Player Piano*

Waugh, Evelyn. *Love Among the Ruins*

Wolfe, Bernard. *Limbo*

Educational Impressions, Inc.

Utopian Communities

Activity No. 11   **Student Work Sheet**

The utopian idea moved to the United States during the last part of the 18th century and the first half of the 19th century. Many experimental communities were begun, but few were very long lasting. Below is an abbreviated list of a few of the communities which were started in America. Choose one of these (or add one of your own) and learn what you can about the community.

Ephrata (1732–1905)

Rappite Settlements (1803–1905)

   Community of Equality

   Harmony

   Economy

Amana Society (1843–1900s)

   Ebenezer and seven other communities

Shakers (1787–1900s)

   New Lebanon and seventeen other settlements in eight states

Oneida Community (1841–1879)

New Harmony (1825–1827)

Fruitlands (19th century)

Brook Farm (19th century)

Morningstar (20th century)

Communes (mid-20th century)

Other ideas worth research are monasteries and convents, the Israeli kibbutzim and shitufim, and farm or other collectives.

Secondary Sources

Activity No. 12

Student Work Sheet

Amis, Kingsley. *New Maps of Hell*

Armytage, W.H.G. *Yesterday's Tomorrows*

Bailey, J.O. Pilgrim's Through Time and Space: *Patterns in Scientific and Utopian Fiction*

Berneri, Marie Louise. *Journey Through Utopia*

Erasmus, Charles J. In Search of the Common Good: *Utopian Experiments Past and Future*

Eurich, Neal. *Science in Utopia: A Mighty Design*

Gerber, Richard. *Utopian Fantasy*

Gray, Donald J. and Allan Orrick. *Designs of Famous Utopias: Materials for Research Papers*

Hertzler, Joyce O. *The History of Utopian Thought*

Manuel, Frank E. *Utopias and Utopian Thought*

Meyer, Karl E. *The New America: Politics and Society in the Age of the Smooth Deal*

Moos, Rudolph and Robert Brownstein. *Environment and Utopia: A Synthesis*

Mumford, Lewis. *The Story of Utopias*

Negley, Gleen and J. Max Patrick. *The Quest for Utopia: An Anthology of Imaginary Societies*

North, Robert C. *The World That Could Be*

Richter, Peyton E. *Utopias: Social Ideals and Communal Experiments*

Russel, Frances Theresa. *Touring America*

Walsh, Chad. *From Utopia to Nightmare*

Weisbrod, Carol. *The Boundaries of Utopias*

Educational Impressions, Inc.